DATE DUE

How does SAND become GLASS?

Melissa Stewart

Chicago, Illinois

an imprint of Capstone Global Library, LLC
Chicago, Illinois

Edited by David Andrews and Laura Knowles
Designed by Richard Parker and Wagtail
Original illustrations © Capstone Global Library, LLC 2010
Illustrated by Jeff Edwards
Picture research by Mica Brancic
Originated by Modern Age Repro House Ltd
Printed and Bound in the United States
by Corporate Graphics

14 13 12 11 10
10 9 8 7 6 5 4 3 2 1

Library of Congress Cataloging-in-Publication Data
Stewart, Melissa.
How does sand become glass? / Melissa Stewart.
p. cm.
Includes bibliographical references and index.
ISBN 978-1-4109-3449-9 (hc) -- ISBN 978-1-4109-3457-4 (pb)
1. Sand, Glass--Juvenile literature. 2. Erosion--Juvenile literature. 3. Glass--Juvenile literature. I. Title.
TN939.S74 2008
666'.1--dc22
2008052654

Acknowledgments

The author and publishers are grateful to the following for permission to reproduce copyright material: Alamy pp. **10** (The London Art Archive), **15** (Yoav Levy), **18** (Diana Mewes), **20** (© Hemis); Corbis pp. **4** (Christoph Wilhelm), **5** (© Peter Arnold, Inc/James L. Amos [Frederic Pitchal]), **14** (Mika/ zefa); Getty Images pp. **7** (Jeff Hunter), **21** (Taxi/Hans Neleman); istockphoto **background image** (© Dean Turner); Photolibrary pp. **8** (Creatas -), **11** (Michael Peuckert), **12** (Jeremy Woodhouse), 16 (Adam Woolfitt), 17 (PAUL NEVIN), **19** (DesignPics Inc.), **22** (Ilker Gurer), **23** (Monty Rakusen), **24** (Jeremy Woodhouse), **26** (Axel M Cipollini), **27** (Animals Animals/BRECK P KENT), **28** (Jean Rey/Photononstop), **29** (Fancy -); Science Photo Library pp. **6** (Raul Gonzalez Perez), **25** (PETER MENZEL).

Cover photograph of sand (top) reproduced with permission of Shutterstock/© Tjerrie Smit and a front view of a glass building (bottom) reproduced with permission of istockphoto/© clu.

Contents

Some words are shown in bold, **like this**. You can find out what they mean by looking in the glossary.

From Sand to Glass

What do a windowpane, a lightbulb, and a pickle jar have in common? They are all made of glass. Glass is a mixture of natural materials. Its most important ingredient is sand.

Believe it or not, the thin, clear sheets of glass in your windows are made from sand.

To make glass, workers shovel the sandy mixture into a **furnace**. The furnace heats the ingredients to about 1,500°C (2,700°F). That is almost eight times hotter than the temperature we use to cook most foods!

As the **solid** sandy mixture heats up, it melts into a soft, gooey **liquid** called **molten** (melted) glass. When molten glass cools, it hardens to form solid glass.

This hot, molten glass is being poured into a mold, where it will cool and become solid.

Think about it!

What common material can be a solid, a liquid, or a **gas** in our everyday world? The answer is water. Ice cubes are solid water, the water that flows out of a faucet is a liquid, and the steam above a whistling teakettle is a gas.

What Is Sand?

You have probably seen sand lots of times. But have you ever looked at it closely? Sand is more interesting than you might think.

When you scoop up sand and rub it between your fingers, how does it feel? Sand feels rough and gritty because it is made of many tiny pieces, or grains. These grains can be rounded or can have jagged edges.

This image shows a tiny grain of sand from the Sahara Desert that has been magnified many times.

No two sand grains look the same. They come in many different colors, shapes, and sizes. Most of the grains are bits of **rock**. Some sand contains tiny pieces of shells, **coral** (the hard material left behind after a coral animal dies), and other materials.

These Bleeker's parrot fish live on a coral reef in the South Pacific Ocean.

Fish that make sand

Parrot fish live on coral reefs all over the world. As the parrot fish hunt for food, they munch on coral with their strong teeth. Then bones in their throats grind the coral into sand. The sand travels through their bodies and leaves as waste material. Believe it or not, we have parrot fish to thank for some of the sandy beaches in warm parts of the world.

Where Is Sand Found?

If you live near a beach or a desert, you probably see sand every day. You can also find sand at the bottom of a stream or on the side of the road. Sand is in most **soil**, too. Soil is a mixture of broken-up **rocks**, rotting plants, and animal material.

This unpaved desert road is made of sand.

The rocky bits in soil come in three sizes. The largest ones are sand. The medium-size ones are called **silt**. Silt is just large enough to see with your eyes. The smallest bits are called **clay**. Plants grow best in soil that has a mixture of all three sizes.

How sandy is the soil near your home? To find out, dig some up and squeeze it. Does it hold together or fall apart?

Add a little water and squeeze it again. What happens? Use the table to find out which kind of soil you have.

	Mostly sand	**Mostly silt**	**Mostly clay**
Dry	Feels gritty, falls apart	Feels smooth and silky, holds together	Feels slippery or sticky, breaks into hard clumps
Wet	Holds together, but crumbles easily	Holds together but cannot be rolled	Holds together and can be rolled

What Are Rocks?

Rocks are natural objects that are made of **minerals**. Minerals are natural **solid** materials. Some rocks contain just one mineral, but most contain two or more minerals.

Thousands of years ago, people made tools from a rock called flint. Flint contains the mineral **quartz**. Today, many buildings and sculptures are made of a rock called granite. Granite contains the minerals quartz, feldspar, and mica.

The people who made these flint tools lived more than 10,000 years ago.

Flint tools

It is no surprise that both flint and granite contain quartz. Most rocks do. Quartz is one of the most common minerals on Earth.

Pure quartz is made of **silica**. The sand used to create glass is made mostly of silica.

Quartz crystals

These beautiful, clear quartz crystals formed slowly over millions of years.

Did you know?

Silica is the most common material in sand. It is also an important material in your body. Silica keeps your skin stretchy. It makes your teeth and bones strong. It even helps your eyes, heart, and lungs do their jobs. Thank goodness for silica!

From Rock to Sand

All the rocky pieces that make up sand start out as much larger **rocks**. Large rocks are hard and tough, but they do not last forever.

Crashing waves are slowly breaking down these rocks in Western Australia.

Strong winds carrying sand and dust slap against rocks and wear away the edges. Pouring rain, crashing waves, and rushing streams smash into rocks and knock off pieces. Ice can break up rock, too.

Make your own sand

To see how water turns rock into sand, all you need is a coffee can with a lid, some clean water, a few small rocks, and a clear plastic cup.

Wash the rocks and coffee can. Then place the rocks in the can, add the water, and snap the lid on. Shake the can for about three minutes.

Remove the lid and pour some water into the glass. The water should look cloudy because it contains tiny bits of rock. If you run your finger along the bottom of the can, you will feel rough, gritty sand.

Keeping It Cool

Here, a worker is reheating a glass **gob** until it is hot enough to mold into a different shape.

Silica is the most common **mineral** in sand. Most of the glass that people make today is about 70 percent silica.

Sand melts at about 1,700°C (3,000°F). Heating sand to such a high temperature would take a lot of energy. To save energy and money, workers add other materials to the sand.

First, they add a white powder called **soda ash**. It comes from plants. Soda ash lowers the melting point of sand to about 1,500°C (2,700°F). But the glass that it makes quickly dissolves, or breaks up, in water. To protect the glass, **limestone** (see box) is added.

A look at limestone

Limestone is a **rock** made from the shells of tiny ocean creatures. People use it to make everything from chalk and concrete to paper and toothpaste. The ancient Egyptians and Mayans used limestone blocks to build their great pyramids.

The glass made from silica, soda ash, and limestone is called "soda glass." It is used to make windows,

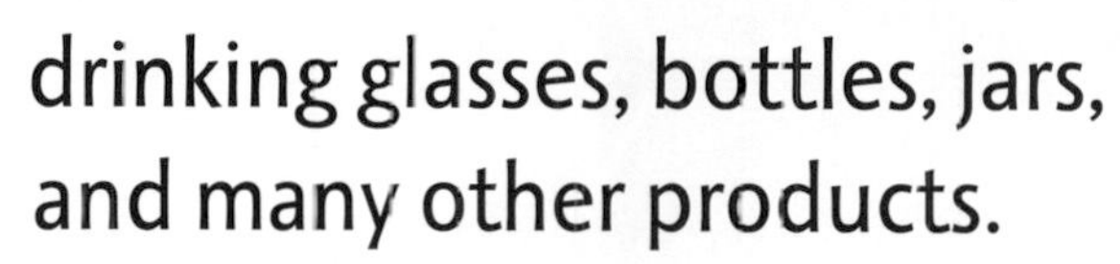

drinking glasses, bottles, jars, and many other products.

Thank goodness for soda glass! It makes the perfect containers for drinking milk, juice, or water.

Glass in the Past

People have been creating glass objects for at least 5,500 years. But no one knows for sure who made glass first.

For a long time, scientists thought the ancient Mesopotamians invented glassmaking. These people lived in the area where Syria, Turkey, and Iraq are today. But new information shows that the ancient Egyptians may have made glass first.

These ancient glass-glazed containers were made by the Mesopotamians 4,000 to 5,000 years ago.

The recipe for making glass has not changed much over time. Ancient peoples used white **quartz** pebbles they found on the ground. They burned plants to get **soda ash**. They ground **limestone** with simple metal tools.

Today, people start the glassmaking process with sand—not pebbles. Some of the sand is ground-up sandstone. This formed over millions of years as layers of sandy **sediment** built up in lakes and seas. As the weight of the top layers pressed down on the lower layers, the sediment stuck together and hardened into stone.

After these workers remove sandstone blocks from a quarry in Australia, machines will grind them into sand.

Workers dig the rest of the sand out of the ground. Layers of heavy sediment did not pile up on top of this sand, so it never turned to stone.

Heating It Up

Soda glass (see page 15) is perfect for making windows, mirrors, and many kinds of containers. It does not cost a lot of money to produce. It is transparent, so light can pass through it. It is clear, so people can see what is on the other side.

But when soda glass heats up or cools quickly, it may crack. That means it cannot be used to make cookware, the glass tubes inside televisions, some kinds of lightbulbs, or test tubes. These products are made from **silica** and a white powder called borax. Borax costs more than **soda ash**, so it is only used for making glass that needs to be heated.

The glass used to make this pot contains borax so that it can be heated enough to boil water.

We take lightbulbs like this one for granted, but we would not be able to make them without glass.

That's electric!

U.S. inventor Thomas Edison created the first lightbulb in 1879. Lightbulbs have been lighting up our world ever since. To make a lightbulb's protective glass cover, a machine puffs air into a small lump of **molten** glass. The air blows up the bulb like your breath blows up chewed bubble gum.

Making Windows

Factories around the world make millions of glass windows every year. Glass is a perfect material for windows because it lets in light and we can see through it. On chilly days, glass windows keep cold air out and warm air in.

These pieces of sheet glass have been made in many different colors.

Window glass is called flat glass or sheet glass. To make it, workers allow **molten** glass to flow into a large pan full of a melted metal called tin. The glass does not mix with the tin. It rests on top of the tin like olive oil rests on top of vinegar in a bottle of Italian salad dressing.

As the molten glass spreads out, it forms a thin, flat sheet. The sheet is cooled very slowly so that the glass does not crack.

People use mirrors every day, from in the bathroom to driving a car. Can you imagine a world without mirrors?

Mirror, mirror

Mirrors are made from a flat sheet of glass. Machines add a coat of silver paint to the back of the glass. Light passes through the glass sheet, but the silver paint reflects (bounces back) the light. When the light comes back through the glass, you see yourself and everything behind you.

Making Bottles and Jars

Glass is also a good material for making bottles, jars, and other kinds of containers. Glass is strong enough to hold all kinds of things. It is clear, so we can see what is inside a glass container. Colorful glass bowls, vases, and drinking glasses can be very beautiful.

This man is blowing through a metal pipe to shape a glass gob. What kind of glass object do you think he will make?

Glass blowing

Blowing and bending

Some people like to shape glass containers by hand. They place a long pipe into a **furnace** and pick up a **gob**. Then they blow into the end of the pipe to hollow out the center. Finally, they use tools to stretch, flatten, or bend the glass into a beautiful object.

When machines make container glass in a factory, balls of **molten** glass called gobs fall into empty molds. In some factories, a stream of air gently blows into each mold to form the container's hollow center. In other factories, a metal plunger presses into each gob to create the container's shape. When the molten glass cools, the molds are flipped over and the new container pops out.

Bottle manufacturing

The machines in this glass factory produce hundreds of bottles every day.

A Line in the Sand

People have been making glass for thousands of years. But nature has been making it for even longer.

Lightning strikes Earth's surface 25 to 30 times every second. Each bolt zaps the ground with 28,000°C (50,000°F) of heat energy. That is five times hotter than the surface of the Sun!

Lightning strikes Earth thousands of times every day, but fulgurite only forms when the conditions are just right.

If a lightning bolt stays in contact with sandy **soil** for about a second, it can melt the **silica**. When the **molten** glass cools, it forms a hollow tube that marks the lightning's path. These glass tubes are called **fulgurites**.

A fulgurite

This amazing piece of a fulgurite branches out in many directions. Its shape gives scientists an idea of how the lightning traveled across the sandy ground.

Fulgurites can be up to 7.5 centimeters (3 inches) across. Some are more than 5 meters (16 feet) long. Fulgurites are very fragile. It is hard to remove them from the ground in one piece.

Imagine that!

By studying fulgurites, scientists can learn how long ago they formed. A Mexican scientist named Rafael Navarro-González recently found a 15,000-year-old fulgurite in the Sahara Desert.

A Blast of Glass

A lightning strike is not the only thing that can cause natural glass to form. A **volcano** can, too.

Each year, people report about 50 volcanoes erupting on Earth. Sometimes lava gently spills out of the volcano and slowly spreads over the land. Other eruptions are more dangerous. Lava, ash, and extremely hot **gases** shoot hundreds of feet into the air.

Mount Etna, Italy

When Italy's Etna volcano blew its top in 2001, lava, ash, and gases blasted high into the air.

The air high in the sky is much cooler than the air near the ground. Cool air makes lava harden quickly. If lava hardens fast enough, it will form a dark, shiny glass called obsidian.

Obsidian is hard and flakes easily. Long ago, people used obsidian to make cutting tools, weapons, and jewelry.

Obsidian

Obsidian can be brown or pink, but it is usually a deep black color.

What is beach glass?

Beach glass is not natural glass. When broken pieces of human-made glass fall into the ocean, powerful waves roll the glass pieces back and forth over sand and rocks. This wears the edges smooth. Then the waves wash the glass onto shore when the tide (rising and falling ocean water) comes in.

Glass and More Glass

It takes a lot of energy to make glass.

- Bulldozers and other machines dig the materials out of the ground.
- Trucks carry the materials to glass factories.
- **Furnaces** burn fuel to melt the ingredients into **molten** glass.
- The machines that shape molten glass use energy, too.

Large dump trucks like this one deliver loads of sand to glass factories.

To help save energy, you and your family can recycle glass. Some glass bottles can be recycled at grocery stores. You can take the rest of your glass containers to recycling centers.

More and more people are beginning to recycle glass, plastic, and aluminum cans. It's amazing how many new products can be made from our used containers.

Broken pieces of recycled glass containers are called cullet. This can be used to make new glass. When glass factories use cullet, they do not need to dig up or haul as much sand.

Recycled glass can also be used to make other kinds of products. One company now makes kitchen countertops and floor tiles out of old glass bottles, mirrors, windshields, and bathtubs.

We use glass in so many ways. It is hard to imagine life without it.

Glossary

clay very small, rocky bits in soil

coral hard material left behind after a coral animal dies

fulgurite hollow glass tube that may form when lightning strikes sand

furnace structure in which heat is produced. A furnace can be used to heat a building or to melt sand, metals, and other materials.

gas substance such as air that spreads to fill any space. Most gases are invisible.

gob ball of molten glass

limestone kind of rock that is ground up and added to soda glass

liquid substance that can be poured. A liquid feels wet, can flow, and takes the shape of the container it is in.

mineral natural solid material

molten melted

quartz common mineral on Earth. Pure quartz, or silica, is one of the main minerals in sand.

rock nonliving object made of one or more minerals

sediment layers of mud, sand, and other materials that slowly build up over time

silica natural substance used to make glass

silt medium-sized rocky bits in soil

soda ash white powder made from plants. It is used to make many kinds of glass because it lowers the melting point of sand.

soil mixture of broken-up rocks, rotting plants, and animal material

solid material that has its own shape and is usually hard

volcano mountain that is made from lava floes at Earth's surface that build up over many eruptions

Find Out More

Books to read

Do you still have questions about glass, sand, and minerals? There is much more to learn about these fascinating topics. You can find out more by picking up some of these books from your local library:

Koscielniak, Bruce. *Looking at Glass Through the Ages*. Boston: Houghton Mifflin Company, 2006.

Prager, Ellen J. *Sand (Jump into Science)*. Washington, D.C.: National Geographic Society, 2006.

Stewart, Melissa. *Extreme Rocks and Minerals! Q&A*. New York: Harper Collins, 2007.

Websites to explore

Check out this article about how the ancient Egyptians made glass:
www.sciencenewsforkids.org/articles/20050629/Note3.asp

Explore this site to learn more about rocks and minerals:
www.minsocam.org/MSA/K12/K_12.html

Want to know more about how rocks form? Take a look at this site:
www.rocksforkids.com/RFK/howrocks.html

Index